5/2013

LAFOURCHE PARISH PUBLIC LIBRARY

0 0533 006!

W9-BXX-707

y

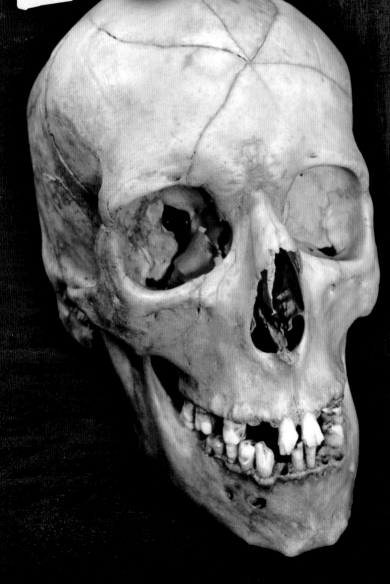

BONES

Titles in the True Forensic Crime Stories series:

BONES
DEAD PEOPLE DO TELL TALES
Library Ed. ISBN 978-0-7660-3669-7
Paperback ISBN 978-1-59845-363-8

CYBERCRIME
DATA TRAILS DO TELL TALES
Library Ed. ISBN 978-0-7660-3668-0
Paperback ISBN 978-1-59845-361-4

DNA AND BLOOD
DEAD PEOPLE DO TELL TALES
Library Ed. ISBN 978-0-7660-3667-3
Paperback ISBN 978-1-59845-362-1

FINGERPRINTS
DEAD PEOPLE DO TELL TALES
Library Ed. ISBN 978-0-7660-3689-5
Paperback ISBN 978-1-59845-364-5

GUN CRIMES
DEAD PEOPLE DO TELL TALES
Library Ed. ISBN 978-0-7660-3763-2
Paperback ISBN 978-1-59845-365-2

TRACE EVIDENCE
DEAD PEOPLE DO TELL TALES
Library Ed. ISBN 978-0-7660-3664-2
Paperback ISBN 978-1-59845-366-9

BONES

TRUE
forensic
CRIME
stories

Dead People DO Tell tales

Sara L. Latta

Lafourche Parish Public Library
Thibodaux, LA

Enslow Publishers, Inc.
40 Industrial Road
Box 398
Berkeley Heights, NJ 07922
USA

http://www.enslow.com

Copyright © 2012 by Sara L. Latta

All rights reserved.

No part of this book may be reproduced by any means
without the written permission of the publisher.

Library of Congress Cataloging-in-Publication Data:

Latta, Sara L.
 Bones : dead people DO tell tales / Sara L. Latta.
   p. cm. — (True forensic crime stories)
 Includes bibliographical references and index.
 Summary: "Uses true crime stories to explain the science of forensics and physical
anthropology"—Provided by publisher.
 ISBN 978-0-7660-3669-7
 1. Forensic anthropology—Case studies—Juvenile literature. I. Title.
 GN69.8.L38 2011
 614.17—dc22

                                  2010011893

Paperback ISBN 978-1-59845-363-8

Printed in China

052011 Leo Paper Group, Heshan City, Guangdong, China

10 9 8 7 6 5 4 3 2 1

To Our Readers: We have done our best to make sure all Internet Addresses in this book were active
and appropriate when we went to press. However, the author and the publisher have no control over
and assume no liability for the material available on those Internet sites or on other Web sites they
may link to. Any comments or suggestions can be sent by e-mail to comments@enslow.com or to the
address on the back cover.

Photo Credits: © 1999 Artville, LLC, p. 60; American Association for the Advancement of Science
Archives/National Library of Medicine, p. 56; Associated Press, pp. 50, 52, 54, 58, 67, 73, 79, 85;
Department of Defense, p. 74; Les Todd/Duke Photography, p. 46; Getty Images Entertainment/
Getty Images, pp. 61, 83; LifeArt image copyright 1998 Lippincott Williams & Wilkins. All rights
reserved, p. 12; © North Wind Picture Archives/Alamy, p. 26; Photo Researchers, Inc.: © Gianni
Tortoli, p. 22, © Martin Shields, pp. 1, 3, © Pascal Goetgheluck, pp. 11, 35, © Pasquale Sorrentino,
p. 13, © Peter Menzel, pp. 32–33, 38, 45; Shutterstock.com, pp. 5, 18–19, 29, 30, 31, 48, 62, 63, 71,
77, 88; U.S. Air Force Photo by Master Sgt. Bill Huntington, p. 6.

Cover Photo: © Martin Shields/Photo Researchers, Inc.

Contents

Metairie, Louisiana, a suburb of New Orleans, was badly damaged during Hurricane Katrina in 2005.

An Introduction to Forensic Anthropology

Lynne Landreneau was worried about her aging father, Leroy Adams. Leroy had gone to live with his son Lon and grandson after Hurricane Katrina destroyed his New Orleans home in August 2005. The hurricane hit the Gulf Coast states with a fury that caused nearly $81 billion in damages and took the lives of over 1,800 people. Landreneau had seen her father during the Christmas holidays that year, although Katrina had made it hard for anyone to feel merry. But after that, every time she called Lon's house to talk with their father, her brother made up some excuse for why he couldn't come to the phone. "He's sleeping," Lon might say. "He's tired. He's not feeling well. He's angry with you and doesn't

want to talk." Finally, she'd had enough. She filed a missing persons report in June 2008.

The deputies searched Lon Adams's home in Metairie, a pleasant suburb of New Orleans. But what they found in a bedroom upstairs was far from pleasant. The remains of someone who had clearly been dead a long time lay on a bare mattress. Detective Todd Giacona said the room had what he called "a Katrina smell: Mildew with a mixture of death."[1] He suspected that they had found Leroy Adams, but the body was so badly **decomposed** that it was impossible to tell.

So the authorities called Mary Manhein, known around those parts as The Bone Lady. Manhein is a **forensic** anthropologist—a scientist who studies human bones to answer legal questions, often in criminal cases. Manhein has seen many bones that bore silent witness to the lives and often-tragic deaths of their owners.

When Manhein and her team from Louisiana State University's Forensic Anthropology and Computer Enhancement Services (FACES) Lab arrived on the scene, they took pictures, made notes, and carefully slid a piece of cardboard under the remains and placed them into a body bag.

Back in their laboratory in Baton Rouge, they examined the bones. From the shape of the pelvis and the skull, they could tell that the remains had belonged to a man. The wear and tear on his bones told them that he had been an old man. The dried-out nature of the bones and little bits of remaining tissue told Manhein that the man had been dead for several months to years. By comparing the man's dental and medical records with his teeth and bones, they soon confirmed that these were the remains of Leroy Adams.

As Manhein and her team prepared to X-ray the skeleton, they noticed some injuries. Several of his ribs, his fingers, a toe, a **vertebra**,

and a U-shaped bone in his neck, the **hyoid**, had been broken. She could tell that these bones had been broken at or around the time of death; the jagged breaks had not yet begun to heal. And she could see where fluids from the decomposing body had seeped into cracks in the bone.

Based in part on the forensic evidence, Lon Adams was charged with murdering his father sometime during the first half of 2006.

At the trial, Adams wept as he confessed that he believed he had accidentally killed his father. "I couldn't admit to myself that I might have accidentally killed daddy," he told the jurors. "I don't think I could have admitted it to anybody else."[2] And so he left his father in the upstairs bedroom of his home. He didn't return to his father's slowly decomposing body for the next two and a half years.

Adams's attorney argued that the old man mostly likely fell out of his bed and onto a nearby footlocker, causing his fatal injuries. The son had simply slipped and fallen on his father's neck while trying to get him back into bed.

Manhein, a witness for the prosecution in Adams's trial, found that scenario highly unlikely. So did Dr. Karen Ross, the medical examiner who determined that Adams had been murdered. "In my opinion," Dr. Ross said at the trial, "I don't see how a fall onto that foot locker would account for all those rib fractures. . . . I think it was intentionally inflicted trauma, either punching or kicking."[3]

In the end, the story the bones told won. The jury found Lon Adams guilty of manslaughter.

What Is Forensic Anthropology?

Forensic **anthropology** uses the scientific study of humans to answer legal questions. "Forensic" comes from a Latin word referring to the forum. The Roman forum was a place where legal issues and politics were discussed and debated. Today, the practice of public speaking and debating is often called forensics. The term **forensic science** has come to mean science used in a court of law or the justice system.

Anthropology is the scientific study of humans and our ancestors. Some anthropologists study languages or cultures. An anthropologist who studies past cultures is an archaeologist. Biological anthropologists specialize in human anatomy and the biology of skeletons. Forensic anthropologists fall into this category. Most adults have 206 bones, but just like **fingerprints**, no two skeletons are alike. To biological anthropologists, the bones tell the story of a person's life—and sometimes death.

When law enforcement officers discover the body of a person who has died from unknown causes, or from a suspected murder or suicide, they call a medical examiner or coroner to help investigate the scene. If the remains are badly decomposed or mutilated, or just a skeleton, the investigators will often ask a forensic anthropologist to help figure out the person's identity and how they died. Many forensic anthropologists have some training in **archaeology**, which makes them valuable in helping investigate crime scenes. They may help dig up buried remains, take photographs and soil samples, or look for footprints and other tell-tale clues at the site. They examine insect activity and chemicals around the body to help determine how long the person has been dead. Once the investigators have thoroughly examined the site, they send the bones and remains to a lab for further study.

Reading the Bones

Imagine that you are a forensic anthropologist. The police have found some bones in a wooded area nearby. They would like you to take a look at them. Your first task is to determine whether the bones are human. Douglas Ubelaker, an anthropologist at the Smithsonian Institution in Washington, D.C., says that between 10 and 15 percent of the bones sent

An anthropology student measures a skull.

to the FBI for investigation are not human at all. For example, the bones of a bear's paw look a lot like those of a human hand. As a biological anthropologist, you have the training that allows you to tell the difference between the bones of animals and humans. If there is any doubt, many physical anthropologists often have collections of animal skeletons to compare with human bones.

Next, you examine the skeleton for clues about the person's sex. The most obvious difference between the bones of males and females is the shape of the pelvis. Men have a narrow, tall pelvis. Women have a wider, shallower pelvis—better for carrying and delivering a baby.

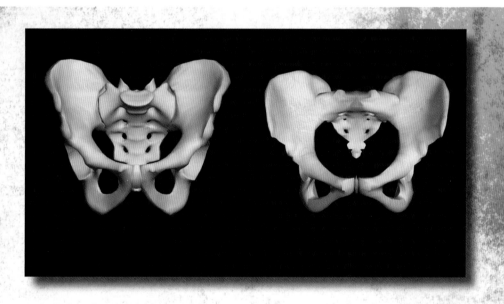

MALE OR FEMALE?

Q: Can you tell the male pelvis from the female pelvis?

A: The narrow, tall pelvis on the left is male; the wider, shallower pelvis on the right is female.

Training in archaeology helps forensic anthropologists learn how to dig up remains. This archaeologist has uncovered a skull.

Because men usually have bigger muscles than women, the areas of the bones where the muscles attach tend to be larger and rougher. You pay special attention to the jaw and brow bones, and the places where the muscles attach at the back of the skull and just behind the ear.

How old was the individual at the time of death? When we are born, we have 300 separate bones. As we grow, some of those bones join, or fuse together. By the time we reach adulthood, we have 206 bones. Because each bone fuses at a predictable rate in most people, the fused and unfused bones can provide valuable clues about the age of the skeleton. The collarbone, for example, fuses between the ages of eighteen and thirty. But the bones that join at the base of the skull fuse completely between twenty and twenty-five years of age. So if you have a skeleton with a fused collarbone but bones that have not yet completely joined at the base of the skull, you can confidently say that the individual was probably between eighteen and twenty-five years of age. Other bones, if you have them, can help you narrow that age range even more. You also look for wear and tear on the bones, especially those in the pelvis, the ribs, and the **vertebrae**. Teeth can be especially useful, particularly in children who have not yet lost all of their baby teeth.

Bones, particularly those in the skull, may also tell you something about an individual's ancestry. You can see by looking at your parents that you have inherited traits from each of them: dark skin or light, kinky or straight hair, or somewhere in between. You inherited your tendency to be long and lanky, or short and squat. These traits were passed down through many generations. Your physical appearance can be traced back to one or more of three major world groups: European, Asian and Native American, or African.

Part of the reason for this variation is that our ancestors didn't travel a lot; they tended to have families with people who lived nearby and had similar physical features. But our ancestors also evolved over the course of thousands of years to adapt to their living conditions. Take skin color, for example. Groups of people who adapted to very warm, sunny parts of the world near the equator, from sub-Saharan Africa to southern India to northern Australia, tended to have very dark skin that would better protect them from the sun's ultraviolet rays. Populations from more northern latitudes tend to have lighter-colored skin, which makes it easier for them to absorb the ultraviolet rays that make it possible for their bodies to make vitamin D.

Bone structure evolved among our ancestors in much the same way. People of African descent, for instance, tend to have wide, short nasal openings, better suited to breathing hot, dry air. The bone around the upper part of the mouth tends to jut out. People of Asian and Native American ancestry often have flat cheekbones, a medium or short nasal opening, and a rounded skull. People of European ancestry usually have a long, narrow nasal opening and a projecting chin. Of course, many of us are of mixed ancestry, so these differences are often blurred. President Obama's ancestry, for example, is half European and half African, and his skeletal structure probably shows traits of both ancestral lines.

Although scientists today have largely abandoned the idea that there are distinct biological "races," forensic anthropologists can and do use skeletal differences to make some inferences about an individual's ancestry.

Now you measure the length of some bones—the most reliable are from the leg. You can plug these measurements, along with information about the individual's sex and ancestry, into a mathematical formula that will help you determine the person's height before death.

So you know the sex, ancestry, approximate age and height of the individual. But the bones can tell you much more about someone's life—and death. Any fillings, crowns, or other dental work can often be matched to dental records. If the teeth show signs of decay or unusual wear, it might be an indication that the individual could not afford to go to the dentist or had poor nutrition. Bony ridges on the wrists might indicate that he worked with his hands for a living. Healed broken bones tell the story of some injury in that person's life. You also look for signs of trauma that happened around the time of death. Are there any bullet holes or knife marks?

Finally, you look for clues that will help you understand what happened to the body after death. This is an area of study called **taphonomy**. Are there bite marks from a coyote or other scavenger? If you were able to visit the site where the body was found, you would check for insects, which can help you estimate how long the individual has been dead. Flies arrive at the body shortly after death and lay their eggs; beetles and wasps come later. Climate and weather conditions can cause the insect clock to slow down or speed up, so you take that into consideration as well. Chemicals left by the decomposing body, and plant growth in and around the remains, can provide valuable clues about what happened to the body after death.

You return the bones and any of the other evidence to the medical examiner and tell the law enforcement officials what you have learned. If the investigators are not able to locate a missing person matching the individual's profile, they may ask for a reproduction of her face. You may work with a forensic artist who creates clay likenesses of the person directly on a reproduction of the skull itself. Or you might take a 3-D X-ray scan of the skull to help you re-create a digital image of the individual. These images, shown on local television stations and printed in newspapers, might prompt someone to come forward and identify the individual.

If the individual was murdered and the case goes to trial, you may be asked to act as an expert witness, where you must be able to back up your testimony with sound scientific data.

The renowned forensic anthropologist William Maples said of the skeletons in his laboratory, "They have tales to tell us, even though they are dead. It is up to me, the forensic anthropologist, to catch their mute cries and whispers, and to interpret them for the living, as long as I am able."[4]

A Case of Mistaken Identity

On June 4, 1959, firefighters in the San Francisco Mountains of southwestern New Mexico discovered a car engulfed in flames. They put the fire out, and sorted through the charred, soggy wreckage. They found a mass of burned flesh, a skull, some other bones, and a few large teeth.

The authorities soon found that the car had belonged to a man named Armando, nicknamed "Squirley" because of the impressive size of his front teeth His brothers-in-law were called in to identify the remains. There could be no doubt, the men said; the teeth must have belonged to poor Squirley.

Not long after Squirley's family buried the remains, Squirley himself wandered into a logging camp just five miles from the place where he was supposed to have died. Hungry and exhausted, Squirley told the sheriff that an electrical fire had broken out under the dashboard of his car. Squirley had been carrying some dynamite caps in his car, so he decided to bail out of the window of his car before the whole thing blew to smithereens. He hit his head, and wandered, confused and lost, until he stumbled upon the logging camp.

So who—or what—was buried in Squirley's coffin?

Squirley told the sheriff that he had been carrying around an old Indian skull that he had found, a porcupine he had shot, and some calf bones. A bone expert from the university confirmed the bones dug up from the grave belonged to an ancient Indian, a porcupine (including its very large front teeth), and a calf. Squirley kept that coffin in his living room until the time came for him to be buried in it—for real, this time.

This story, although true, would probably never happen today. In the 1950s, law enforcement officials did not routinely call bone experts to examine remains. The discipline of forensic anthropology simply did not exist.[5] Fortunately, today things have changed.

In June 1959, firefighters found a mysterious car on fire.

2
The Murderous Beginnings of Forensic Anthropology

r. George Parkman left his Walnut Street home in Boston promptly on the morning of November 23, 1849. Parkman was a tall, angular man, familiar to Boston society. This particular day, he was dressed in a dark frock coat and pants, purple vest, and stovepipe hat. Parkman was a wealthy man who specialized in treating mentally ill patients. He donated land to Harvard University where the new medical school would be built. He gave free medical care and money to many of Boston's poor immigrants.

These days, however, he spent most of his time overseeing his many properties and collecting rent from his tenants. He also ran a very profitable money-lending business. And when it came to business debts, the sharp-chinned Parkman—people called him "Chin" behind his back—was notoriously unforgiving. Today, he had a 1:30 appointment to collect a debt from a Harvard professor of chemistry, Dr. John Webster.

Webster was a fun-loving, plump man, as careless with his money as Parkman was careful. Webster had borrowed over $2,000 from Parkman to cover his debts. Though they had once been friends, Parkman suspected that Webster would never repay him. He vowed he'd collect his money that very day.

First, though, Parkman stopped to buy some lettuce for his daughter, who was ill. He thought that some greens, no matter that they were expensive at that time of year, would do her good. He walked to another store, where he placed an order for more groceries to be delivered to his home. He left the lettuce on the counter, saying that he would be back to pick it up in a few minutes. Two schoolboys spotted Parkman striding toward the Medical College.

That evening, Parkman's lettuce lay wilting on the counter of the grocery store. He never returned home. Mrs. Parkman was worried; her husband was never late. She contacted her brother-in-law, who posted notices of his disappearance in flyers and newspapers across the city. They offered a $3,000 reward—an enormous sum of money at the time—for anyone with information leading to his discovery.

The police questioned Webster, who said that he had indeed met with Parkman in his office on Friday afternoon. "I paid him the debt I owed," he insisted, saying that Parkman had hurried out of his office soon after.[1] Webster had never really been a suspect, and the police had no reason to doubt him.

Ephraim Littlefield, the janitor at the medical school, had his own suspicions. He and his wife lived in the basement of the medical college, right next to Webster's laboratory, and he had never really gotten along with Webster. "He had always been at me like some yapping

Physical anthropologists can use remains from a wide variety of time periods in their research. This anthropologist is measuring a skull that's 2,500 years old!

dog: Littlefield, did you leave the windows open again; Littlefield, have you been playing cards in my room again?"[2] But shortly after Parkman's disappearance, Webster gave Littlefield a Thanksgiving turkey—something he had never done before.

Littlefield decided to do a little sleuthing. He knew the building and its secret hiding places well. On a hunch, he went down to a vault under Webster's office the day after Thanksgiving. Webster had the only key to the chamber, so Littlefield hacked through the brick wall, his wife keeping watch above. Peering inside, he saw part of a body hanging from a hook, and "a pelvis . . . some pieces of leg. . . . Perhaps I was expecting a body; perhaps nothing, but not these bits of butcher's trash sitting on the wet dirt. They were so white, you see, so clean and white."[3]

Littlefield was no scientist, but he knew a thing or two about human bones. It was his job to clean up the anatomy laboratory where the students dissected **cadavers**. And he had a little side-business of selling dead bodies stolen from fresh graves to medical students, an activity that led others to dub him a "resurrection man."

Littlefield called the authorities, who did a thorough search of the vault and Webster's office. They found a breastbone and ribs hidden in a tea chest. There was a set of false teeth in the oven Webster used to heat chemicals. They found a burned bone and a button in the furnace. In all, there were 150 bones or bone fragments scattered throughout Webster's office. Some had been burned; others still held the stink of decay. That evening, Webster was arrested and charged with the murder of George Parkman.

The police called in a team of doctors, professors of anatomy, and dentists to examine the remains. One of the experts was a professor of anatomy at Harvard, Dr. Jeffries Wyman. Although his specialty was animal anatomy, he helped piece together Parkman's bones. Another expert was Oliver Wendell Holmes Sr., dean of the Harvard Medical College (and father of Oliver Wendell Holmes Jr., who would one day become a Justice of the U.S. Supreme Court). The investigators concluded that the remains were clearly those of a human, about the same size and age as Parkman. They ruled out a grisly student prank involving one of the dissection cadavers, which would have smelled of embalming fluid.

At the trial, the testimony of Parkman's dentist and friend, Dr. Nathan Keep, clinched the case against Webster. Keep had made Parkman a pair of dentures four years earlier. The Chin's lower jaw was so unusual that Keep had to make special molds to make the dentures. He had kept the mold, just in case Parkman ever needed another pair of dentures. On the witness stand, Keep showed how the false teeth fit his molds exactly.

Webster was found guilty of murder, and sentenced to hang. Before he died, he admitted to killing Parkman by hitting him over the head with a sturdy piece of wood. As his laboratory furnace was too small to burn an entire body, he planned to burn it one piece at a time.

The Legacy

All of Boston was transfixed by the sensational murder trial of John Webster. Thomas Dwight, a seven-year-old boy from Boston, must have grown up listening to stories about how Parkman's bones helped convict Webster. Dwight went to medical school and devoted his career to the study of anatomy at Harvard. He showed how an expert could determine characteristics like sex, age, height, or ancestry from just a few bones. Although he never testified in any high-profile court cases, he wrote a groundbreaking paper, "The Identification of the Human Skeleton: A Medicolegal Study." His research has earned him the title of "The Father of Forensic Anthropology."[4] One of Dwight's students was George Dorsey, who would play an important part in another sensational murder case.

The Sausage Maker's Wife

Everyone knew that Adolph Luetgert made the best sausages in Chicago. Visitors to the German restaurant during the 1893 World's Fair in Chicago raved about the delicious sausages, said to be of "surpassing juiciness and flavor . . . served with sauerkraut. No man who had eaten those frankfurters could fail to remember them—and they were of Luetgert's make."[5] Encouraged by his success, Luetgert built a large house and an even larger new sausage factory next door. His wife, Louisa, thought they should be saving their money, not spending it on a fancy new house and factory. But Adolph didn't listen to her.

Adolph had married Louisa, a pretty, petite woman, sixteen years earlier. He had given her an unusual 18-carat gold wedding ring engraved with her initials, "L.L." But from the beginning their marriage was a stormy one. Their neighbors suspected Luetgert of beating Louisa.

Not long after the World's Fair, the economy took a downturn. People didn't have as much money to spend on sausages. To make things worse, a con man cheated Luetgert out of thousands of dollars. By 1897, Luetgert was deeply in debt. He shut down the factory for remodeling and laid off most of his workers. Louisa continued to blame her husband's big spending for their financial mess. Adolph began sleeping in the factory.

On March 11, 1897, Adolph ordered 378 pounds of potash, a compound made from wood ashes and water. Potash, which was commonly used to make soap, is highly acidic. It can burn or dissolve human flesh. On April 24, he ordered two of his employees to empty the potash into barrels alongside a vat in his factory. Frank Odorowsky, who worked in the smokehouse, said that the potash burned his skin like fire.

Later that day, Luetgert and another employee poured the potash into the vat and filled it with water. It simmered, like a witch's cauldron, for a week.

This woodcut depicts visitors to the Chicago World's Fair in 1893.

On May 1, Adolph sent his factory watchman on two errands that took him out of the factory. That was the last day Louisa Luetgert was seen alive. Later, neighbors reported seeing Louisa and Adolph going into the sausage factory that night. At first, Adolph told people that his wife had gone to visit her sister.

Six days later, her brother reported her missing to the police. Suspicious, they searched the sausage factory. They found a huge vat of some greasy, foul-smelling substance. Luetgert explained that it was simply a mixture of chemicals, animal fat, and scraps of animal bones. He'd been trying to make soap to clean his factory, he said, although he admitted he hadn't been very successful.

When the police officers drained the vat, they found a few small bone fragments, a piece from a woman's undergarment, and two gold rings. One of the rings was a wedding band engraved with the initials "L.L." Later, they found some ashes outside the building containing a few more bone fragments.

Adolph Luetgert was charged with murdering and boiling his wife's remains in a chemical solution. With nearly all of her body dissolved into a greasy jelly, how could Luetgert be proven guilty?

At the trial, Luetgert said his wife must have left him because she was so unhappy with their marriage. She would turn up sooner or later, he was sure. The rings, he said, were too small for his wife's fingers. And the bone fragments? "Laughing heartily until his big cheeks shook," the newspaper report read, "Luetgert held up a fragment said to be a part of his wife's shoulder blade. "'This is a bit of a cow's shoulder bone,'" he said.[6]

Luetgert's defense attorney found witnesses who claimed they had seen Louisa at a railroad station 50 miles away. The jury could not come to a decision, so the judge dismissed them and called for another trial.

In the second trial, both sides brought in bone experts. W.H. Allport, professor of anatomy at Northwestern University Medical School, testified for the defense. Allport said that there was no way of identifying any of the bones as human. He confidently said that one of the bones was definitely from a hog. The lawyer for the prosecution decided to test Allport's knowledge of bones. He pulled some bones out of a paper bag and asked Allport to identify them. Allport examined the bones for about ten minutes. They had belonged to a dog, he said.

No, he was told. He'd been examining the arm and hand of a monkey. "Well, it might be a dog monkey," Allport retorted. "They look a good deal alike."[7] After that, poor Allport began to fall apart. The thigh of a musk ox was that of a hog. He said that a gorilla leg bone had belonged to a man. After a while, he gave the same answer to just about every question: "I don't know."

One of the experts for the prosecution was George A. Dorsey, a curator at the Field Museum in Chicago. Anthropology was a young science then—Dorsey was the first person to graduate from Harvard with a doctoral degree in the field. He had spent his career studying ancient human remains, and was considered an expert in determining a skeleton's sex.

The case came down to four bone fragments, so tiny that all of them would fit on a quarter. The bones, Dorsey said, were a piece of a bone from her hand, a bit of rib, and parts of bones from her toe and foot. All of them, he said, had undoubtedly come from a human female. So convincing was he that those four tiny bones, along with the wedding ring and the suspicious circumstances surrounding Louisa's disappearance, were enough to convince the jury. Luetgert was sentenced to life in prison. He died of a heart attack in prison a year later, still protesting his innocence.

RUMORS

Although the sausage factory was shut down at the time of Louise's disappearance, rumors sprang up that Luetgert had turned his wife into sausage. In big cities all over the United States, sausage sales plummeted. One butcher said that his customers demanded to see proof of his living wife before buying his sausage! Children were soon chanting a new jump rope rhyme:

Old man Luetgert made sausage out of his wife!
He turned on the steam,
His wife began to scream,
There'll be a hot time in the old town tonight![8]

Looking back, Clyde Snow, one of the world's leading forensic anthropologists, wrote that it is unlikely that an anthropologist could determine the sex of a skeleton from just a few tiny pieces of bone. Nevertheless, the Luetgert case marked an important milestone for forensic anthropology. It was the first legal case in which an anthropologist was called upon to testify as an expert witness.

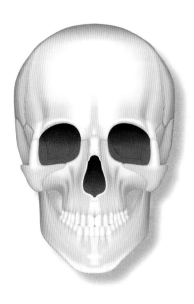

The Body Farm

Corpses are scattered about on a peaceful, wooded parcel of land enclosed by a tall fence topped with razor wire. Just a few miles from downtown Knoxville, Tennessee, the bodies lie buried in shallow graves, submerged in ponds, or stuffed into the trunks of cars. Some are crawling with **maggots**, swathed in the sickly sweet smell of decaying flesh. Others are little more than a pile of dry bones and a mat of hair.

Is it the scene of a mass murder? No, welcome to the Body Farm, more formally known as the University of Tennessee Anthropological Research Facility. The corpses were all donated to the Body Farm by the families of the dead, with the understanding that the remains of their loved ones could help scientific research. Here at the Anthropological Research Facility, the dead *do* tell tales—*if* you understand the language of the bones. This is where students and scientists come to learn more about what happens to a human body after death—the science of taphonomy.

Forensics trainees dug up this skeleton at the Body Farm in Tennessee to see how it had decomposed.

What Happens to a Body After Death?

Immediately after death, the body begins to cool about 1.5 degrees Fahrenheit per hour, until it reaches the temperature of its surroundings. This can vary if the surrounding temperature is very hot or very cold. A few hours after death, chemical changes in the muscles cause the body to stiffen. **Enzymes**—proteins that specialize in splitting other compounds for the body to use—begin to break down cells in the body. Soon, tissues turn to liquid. The body's normal bacteria find themselves awash in a bountiful supply of food. They grow and multiply. As they eat, they produce gas as a waste product. The body, especially the abdomen, becomes bloated. The bloat gradually subsides as the bacteria stop producing gas. The body, like the Wicked Witch of the West in *The Wizard of Oz*, begins to dissolve. Fluids drain from the body and seep into the surrounding soil.

Meanwhile, insects have been busy feasting on the body. Female flies arrive minutes after death and lay their eggs around wounds and natural body openings such as the mouth and eyes. The eggs hatch within twenty-four hours, and the larvae, or maggots, move into the body and feed on the decaying tissue. A second wave of insects, attracted by the smell, begins to arrive. Beetles feed on the maggots and the decaying flesh. Certain kinds of wasps lay their eggs on or inside the maggots.

As body fluids begin to seep into the soil and the corpse dries out, mites and other beetle species begin to move in. The remaining maggots migrate out of the body. They form a hardened shell and enter the **pupa** stage, where they will develop into flies again. When they emerge from their shells, they leave their casings behind, near the remains of the body.

Eventually, after the enzymes, bacteria, various types of insects, and perhaps scavenging animals have done their work, all that remains is a dry pile of bones. This sequence of events is very predictable, no matter where the body decomposes. What can vary is the timing—and the main

This scientist is examining a beetle found on a corpse. You can see the beetle's head on the monitor.

thing that affects the timing is temperature. Bacteria and insects are both more active at warmer temperatures. The entire decomposition process can take as little as two weeks in a warm, humid climate. Climate and soil conditions can slow down or even stop the decay process. Bodies in the desert lose their water so quickly that they become mummified. The 5,300-year-old body of "The Iceman" has been so well preserved by wind and below-zero temperatures high in the Alps that even his eyeballs are intact.

After studying the decomposition of hundreds of bodies, scientists at the Body Farm came up with a mathematical formula that uses weather data at the crime scene to calculate time since death with great accuracy.

The Case of Colonel William Shy

The Body Farm came about because of an embarrassing incident in identifying human remains. In 1977, Dr. Bill Bass, a well-respected forensic anthropologist for the state of Tennessee, got a phone call from Detective Jeff Long. Someone—no one knew who—had dug up the grave of Colonel William Shy, a soldier in the Civil War. Inside the coffin lay a headless corpse. Judging from its still-pink flesh, the remains appeared to be fairly recent. Investigators suspected that the body of Colonel Shy had been stolen, and replaced with the corpse of a murder victim. What better place to hide a body than an old grave? They guessed that the murderer had been scared away before finishing the task of burying the victim.

After examining the gravesite and the body, Dr. Bass concluded that the victim had been dead for no more than a year. But further investigation revealed that the body was indeed that of Colonel William Shy. By analyzing the tissues of the corpse, they found that the soldier's body had been embalmed, or treated with preservatives to prevent decay. And the cast iron coffin in which he was buried had been sealed so tightly that it kept at bay the insects and bacteria that normally break down the soft tissues of a corpse. Grave robbers in search of Civil War relics had dug up his remains. Dr. Bass had misjudged the time since death by over one hundred years![1]

Dr. Bass realized that while he knew a lot about the human skeleton, he and other forensic scientists understood very little about what happens to the human body after death. What effect do climate and weather have on the rate of decomposition? How does one body lying on a forest floor decay differently from another tethered to a block of cement at the bottom of a lake? What can the insects in and around the body tell us about the time since death—often a critical detail in many murder cases? Since **pathologists** cannot perform a normal **autopsy** on bodies that have already begun to decompose, these are questions for forensic anthropologists to answer.

Dr. Bass decided that forensic anthropologists needed a laboratory where they could conduct experiments on their subjects. He persuaded administrators at the University of Tennessee to give him an acre of land near the campus. In 1981, he built a simple storage shed, a strong security fence around his acre, and laid a donated corpse on a concrete slab. And so the Anthropological Research Facility was born.

In the years since, Dr. Bass and his colleagues have studied the decomposition of bodies under a wide range of conditions. They bury the bodies in shallow graves in the woods, stuff them in the trunks of cars, or submerge them in water. They note everything that happens to the bodies, from the time the fresh corpses arrive at the Body Farm until they are nothing more than a pile of bones. Dr. Bass's goal was to create a sort of decomposition database. "Any time a real-life murder victim was found, under virtually any circumstances or at any stage of decomposition, I wanted to be able to tell police—with scientific certainty—when that person was killed," Bass said.[2]

Dr. Bill Bass founded the Body Farm research facility in Tennessee. These students are training to be forensic scientists.

Students, professors, police officers, and FBI agents have all come to the Body Farm to learn more about what happens to the human body after death.

Insect Witnesses

By 1999, Dr. Bass had been studying the decomposition of bodies at the Body Farm for nearly twenty years. He and his colleagues had carried out experiments on the decomposition of over three hundred corpses, under every imaginable condition. When he got a call from a Mississippi district attorney's office in 1999 to help solve a case in which establishing time of death was critical, he was pretty confident that he was up to the challenge. He was soon going to find out just how difficult that would be.

On November 5, 1993, Darrell and Annie Perry, and their four-year-old daughter Krystal, left their suburban New Orleans home for a much-needed getaway. The couple had been having problems.

FORDISC

Even after a research project is finished, the bones at the Body
Farm make one last—and very important—contribution to
forensic science. The scientists clean the bones, measure them,
and enter all of the information about the bones into a database
created by Richard Jantz, an anthropologist at the University of
Tennessee. The scientists enter any other information they have
about the individuals: where they were born, how old they were
when they died, medical history, even what they did for a living. As of 2005, the Forensic Data Bank contains information on
nearly 2,900 skeletons.[3]

The data bank is the heart of a computer program called
FORDISC (Forensic Discrimination), now the world's leading
database of modern human skeletons. Using FORDISC, a forensic
anthropologist can enter a few skeletal measurements from
an unknown crime victim and the computer can estimate the
ancestry, sex, and height of the person.

FORDISC played an important role in helping to identify a
victim of the crash of Flight 93 in Pennsylvania on September
11, 2001. The remains of the victims of 9/11 were often so small
that the best way of identifying them was to compare the DNA
in the bone fragments, if possible, with those of living relatives.
One family lost two daughters in the crash of Flight 93—one was
in her teens, the other was five years old. DNA analysis on some
bones showed that they had belonged to one of the daughters,
but which one? Forensic anthropologists using FORDISC were able
to determine that the bones had come from the older daughter.[4]

They needed some time to sort things out. Darrell's stepfather, Mike Rubenstein, had generously offered to drive them to his secluded cabin nearby, where they could stay as long as they needed. Mike had checked on the cabin twice in the month of November, he said, but both times it was dark and locked.

When he let himself into the cabin on December 16 with a spare key, he found the bodies of Darrell and Annie lying on the living room floor. Krystal's body lay on a bed in the next room. All three of the bodies were already badly decomposed, bloated and crawling with maggots. The medical examiner determined that Darrell and Annie had been stabbed to death; Krystal died of strangulation.

Lead investigator Allen Applewhite soon discovered something even more chilling. Just twenty-four hours after reporting the death of Darrell, Annie, and Krystal to the police, Rubenstein had filed a life-insurance claim for a quarter of a million dollars on his four-year-old granddaughter. When Applewhite investigated the claim, he learned that Rubenstein and Darrell's mother, Doris, had taken out the $250,000 policy on their granddaughter two years earlier. Her death had occurred just three months after the two-year waiting period for benefits. There seemed to be a clear motive for the killing, but there was no hard evidence that could link Rubenstein to the murders. No fingerprints, footprints, bloody knife—nothing. The district attorney refused to prosecute the case.

But the memory of the little girl and her parents haunted Applewhite. He found that two of Rubenstein's acquaintances had also come to mysterious, unfortunate ends. Both times, Rubenstein stood to benefit from their deaths. Finally, in 1999, Applewhite convinced the district attorney's office to prosecute Rubenstein for the murder of his stepson, his stepson's wife, and their daughter. The case went to trial in June of that year.

Rubenstein had an airtight alibi for the two weeks before the bodies were found. If the defense could prove that the family had been alive during that period, then Rubenstein would go free. Establishing the time of death was critical to the case. The chief witnesses, it seemed, would be the maggots found on the bodies of the victims.

Applewhite sent Dr. Bass detailed photographs of the victims' bodies. All three were in an advanced stage of bloat. He could see from the dark, greasy stains that the bodies had begun to liquefy. Knowing that the timing of the decomposition process can vary according to the climate, Dr. Bass asked for the temperature readings for the months of November and December of 1993. The records showed that it had been a pretty chilly fall for Mississippi. Based on the temperature data, Dr. Bass found that the family had been killed somewhere between twenty-five and thirty-five days before they were found—mid-November.

But something puzzled him. The maggots in the photos appeared to be in the third and final growth stage before turning into pupae. This meant that they would have hatched from eggs about two weeks earlier. He didn't see any empty pupa casings, either. The maggots could only tell him that the murders had happened at least two weeks before the bodies were found—December 2.

At the trial, Dr. Bass acknowledged that the maggot story didn't quite fit with the decomposition story. But he also noted that the cabin was tightly built. It could have taken some time for flies outside to detect the smell of death, and even longer to find their way inside the cabin. This made sense to Dr. Bass—but would it make sense to the jury?

Dr. Bass waited and worried as the trial continued. And then, in a stunning turn of events, the maggot pupae made an appearance. A pathologist from the county medical examiner's office took the stand for the defense. She showed a close-up photo of Krystal's face and head. Dr. Bass had never been shown these photos—and what he saw stunned him. "You've got to stop this trial," he whispered to the prosecuting attorney. "You've got to put me back on the stand."[5]

The enlarged photo clearly showed empty pupa casings scattered amidst the roots of the girl's hair. It was clear that the blowflies had begun laying their eggs more than two weeks before the bodies were discovered. Krystal and her parents were already dead by December 2—the earliest date for which Rubenstein had an alibi.

The jury found Rubenstein guilty of three counts of first-degree murder. He received a sentence of life in prison for the murder of Darrell and Annie, and a death sentence for the murder of Krystal. In October 2009, the Mississippi Supreme Court overturned the death penalty because a judge had failed to tell the jurors they could have sentenced Rubenstein to life without parole. He is now serving a sentence of three life terms.[6]

A Prehistoric Murder Mystery

This much is clear: In the mountains of what is now Iraq, a male, roughly forty years old, took a hit to the torso that left him mortally wounded. With the weapon still stuck in his ribs, he made his way to a cave, where he died at least two weeks later.

Fast-forward about 50,000 years, to the year 1960. Archaeologists had unearthed nine Neanderthal skeletons at Shanidar Cave, in the Zagros Mountains of northeastern Iraq. The strong, sturdy Neanderthals, a species that shared an ancestor with *Homo sapiens* (modern humans), lived in Europe and parts of Asia for thousands of years. They used fire, made stone tools, lived in social groups, and buried their dead. They lived at the same time and in the same areas as some modern humans before going extinct, around 30,000 years ago. Did they interbreed with early modern humans and simply disappear as a distinct species? Did they fail to compete for scarce food and resources? Or did humans hunt them to extinction?

READING THE BONES: HOW THEY DIED

It is not always possible for a forensic anthropologist to determine how someone died. The bones of an old man who died peacefully in his sleep reveal nothing about his final moments. But forensic anthropologists are very good at reading the clues to trauma that damages bones. Blunt-force trauma—most commonly occurring as a result of an automobile accident—is the fifth most common cause of deaths in the United States. But it is also the type of trauma most often seen when somebody has been murdered. Baseball bats, tire irons, and frying pans may leave a distinctive imprint on the victim's bones that are a sure giveaway to forensic anthropologists. (Roald Dahl wrote a famous short story in which a woman kills her husband with a frozen leg of lamb, then roasts and serves it to the police who come to investigate the death.)

Knives or machetes cause sharp-force trauma. Anything with a cutting edge will slice through bone, leaving behind clean edges. A broken hyoid bone, a tiny, horseshoe-shaped bone in the throat, almost always means that the victim was strangled to death. A bullet to the skull may leave characteristic entry and exit holes. The size and shape of the holes are clues to the type of gun used and at what range it was fired.

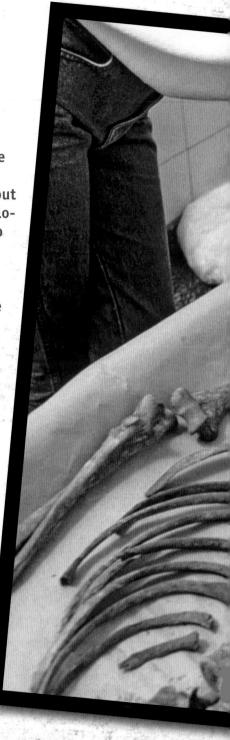

Stephen Churchill holds replicas of Stone Age weapons. He used similar replicas to figure out how the Neatherthal called Shanidar 3 died.

Scientists are still puzzling over the fate of the Neanderthal species, but they have some clues about the demise of one of the Neanderthals in Shanidar Cave. Now called Shanidar 3, he was a forty- to fifty-year-old male with signs of arthritis and a sharp, deep slice in his left ninth rib.

"People have been speculating about the rib injury for going on forty years now," said Steven Churchill, an associate professor of evolutionary anthropology at Duke University.[7] Some speculated that it had been a

hunting accident. Perhaps another Neanderthal had killed him. Or was it an early modern human?

Churchill attempted to answer those questions through a set of experiments that combined modern forensic analysis with Stone Age technology. Neanderthals relied on heavy spears and stone knives, using great strength to drive their weapons into enemies and the animals they hunted. Early modern humans, on the other hand, used lighter weight spear-throwers that allowed them to wield their weapons from a distance. Churchill rigged up a special crossbow to fire replicas of Stone Age arrowheads at pig carcasses obtained from a nearby slaughterhouse. (The skin and bones of Neanderthals are believed to be about as tough as those of pigs.) He also calculated the impact of using a knife or the kind of thrusting spear the Neanderthals used. Then he compared the damage to the ribs of the pigs to the Neanderthal's rib.

Churchill found that Neanderthal thrusting spears caused more massive rib damage than Shanidar 3 had suffered. Whatever had sliced into his rib entered Shanidar 3's body at a 45-degree downward angle—consistent with either a knife or a thrown weapon. But based on modern forensic studies aimed at protecting police officers and prison guards, Churchill knew that knife wounds from that angle tend to produce greater damage to the bone. The Neanderthal's wound was more consistent, he said, "with a light-weight, long-range projectile weapon."[8]

We may never know why Shanidar 3 was killed. But the evidence points to the identity of the killer—an early modern human.

> *"Flesh decays, bone endures. Flesh forgets and forgives ancient injuries; bone heals, but it always remembers: a childhood fall, a barroom brawl; the smash of a pistol butt to the temple, the quick sting of a blade between the ribs."*[9]
>
> — Dr. William Bass

Human Rights

n 1976, it was dangerous to speak out against the government of Argentina after military rulers seized power from President Isabel Perón. Terrorists, riots, and a crumbling economy had placed the country in great turmoil. After the election, the new ruling body, or *Junta*, vowed to restore order to the country. The "Dirty War," as they called their effort to clamp down on their political enemies, soon expanded to just about anyone who dared to disagree with their policies. Thousands of men, women, and children suspected of being troublemakers were kidnapped and taken to detention centers, where they were often tortured for weeks or months before being killed.

This left the *Junta* with the problem of getting rid of the bodies. They returned some of the dead to their families. These they claimed had killed themselves or were caught in a gun battle with police. Some of their victims were drugged and dumped from airplanes into the shark-ridden waters of the South Atlantic Ocean. Others were stripped of all identification and buried in "No Name" (NN) graves. As far as the

Junta were concerned, bones were bones. All of these people came to be known as *desaparecidos*, or "disappeared ones." For their families, it was as though they had vanished into thin air.

The Dirty War finally ended in late 1983, when Argentina elected a new president, Raúl Alfonsin. "Today public immorality has ended," Alfonsin said at his inaugural address. "We are going to build a decent government."[1] He pledged to investigate the disappearances and punish those responsible. The date—December 10, 1983—was International Human Rights Day. Alfonsin quickly formed a commission to investigate the fate of the disappeared ones. Six months later, the commission released a report with the names of 8,961 *desaparecidos* and a list of the military officers believed to be involved in the disappearances.

Judges ordered hundreds of NN graves to be dug up. With little knowledge or skills in forensic anthropology, workers used bulldozers and shovels to dig up NN graves. Human rights lawyers knew that it would be impossible to recover any useful forensic evidence from the piles of jumbled and broken bones. They needed forensic experts to help with the exhumations. But they knew they could not trust some of the Argentine forensic experts, because they had been working with the *Junta* to help cover up these crimes. Others were afraid to take part in the investigations, because if the military came back into power, they were likely to be among the next round of disappeared ones.

The commission knew that it needed to bring in an outside expert. That person was Clyde Snow. A tall Oklahoman who favored cowboy hats and cowboy boots, Snow was one of the leading forensic anthropologists in the United States. He had helped piece together charred and broken bodies from plane crashes, identify the victims of a serial killer, and put names to the fallen soldiers at Custer's Last Stand. If anyone could read the stories of the bones of the disappeared ones, it was Snow.

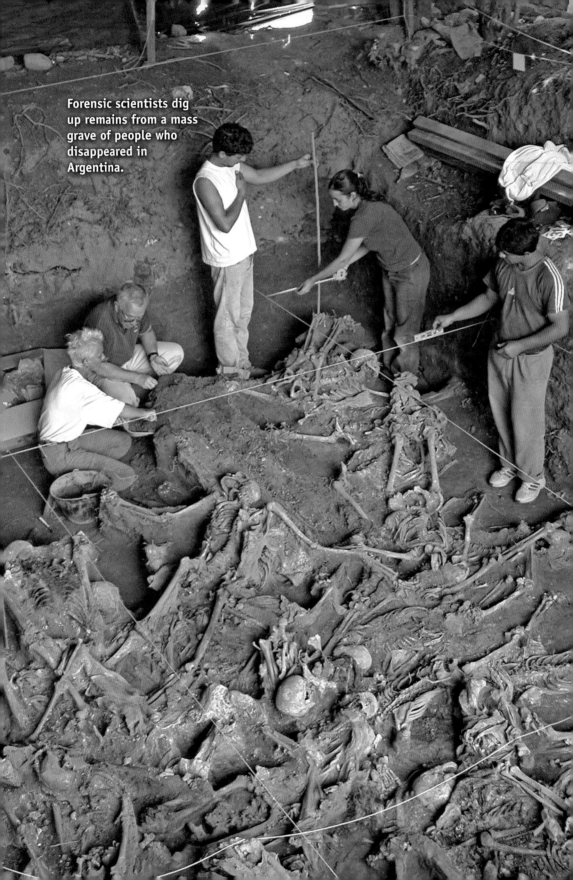

Forensic scientists dig up remains from a mass grave of people who disappeared in Argentina.

Speaking at a 1984 science meeting about the role forensic scientists could play in investigating human rights abuses, Snow said "The great mass murders of our time have accounted for no more than a few hundred victims. In contrast, states that have chosen to murder their own citizens can usually count their victims by the carload lot. As for motive, the state has no peers, for it will kill its victim for a careless word, a fleeting thought, or even a poem."

And then Snow threw down the gauntlet: "Maybe it's time for the forensic scientists of the world to heed the old call of our favorite fictional prototype: 'Quick, Watson, the game's afoot!'—and go after the biggest game of all."[2] Snow was on a plane for Argentina just a few weeks later.

Clyde Snow managed to find a small group of anthropology and medical students who were interested in helping identify the disappeared. They had no experience in forensic anthropology, but they were willing to learn. They dug up their first bodies on such short notice that they had to use improvised tools including wooden chopsticks from a Chinese restaurant and spoons. Snow and his team began work on a chilly June morning as Argentine police—the same ones who terrorized citizens on behalf of the *Junta* just a year earlier—and the family of the woman believed to be buried in the NN grave looked on.

The team excavated the grave just as they would a prehistoric site. First, they used string to map the gravesite into a grid. That way, they could reconstruct the exact location in the grave of each piece of evidence uncovered. Carefully, one spoonful at a time, they dug up the grave. Finally, they reached the skull. It was marked by a bullet-sized hole.

"While she was still in the ground," Snow said, "This woman was telling us she had died of a gunshot wound."[3]

It was sundown by the time they had finished excavating the woman's bones. By midnight they had identified the body from dental records. The remains were not those of the woman in question, but the judge was

Forensic anthropologist Dr. Clyde Snow

impressed. Perhaps it *would* be possible to identify the remains of the disappeared after all.

Clyde Snow soon flew back to the United States, only to return the following year with a second team of forensic scientists. The team was to teach a month-long crash course in forensic science. Snow showed the students how to recover, clean, and preserve bones, and how to read them to determine the victim's sex, age, and stature.

Dr. Lowell J. Levine, a forensic dentist, taught the students how to compare the victim's teeth with dental records and X-rays made before death. Forensic pathologist Robert H. Kirschner showed them how to recognize the different types of gunshot wounds and evidence of torture. Forensic radiologist John Fitzpatrick taught the students how X-rays could be used to help identify victims.

Over the course of the workshop, the scientists and students exhumed the remains of several disappeared ones. One of them would forever change the way that we investigate human rights violations.

Dental evidence is ofen used in forensics.
It may even help identify a person.

Liliana's Story

Liliana Pereyra was twenty-one years old and a bank clerk in the city of Mar de la Plata. Something of a free spirit, she had been active in a student organization that opposed the *Junta*. In October 1976, a witness saw two men in military uniforms grab Liliana and her boyfriend Eduardo and shove them into waiting cars. Liliana was five months pregnant.

Nine months after the kidnapping, Liliana's mother, Coche Pereyra, received a brief notice from the police. Her daughter had been killed, it said, in a shoot-out with the military. She had been buried in an anonymous grave. End of story: there was no further official information. But a fellow prisoner who made it out alive told Coche that her daughter had been tortured at a secret detention center before giving birth to a baby boy. After that, the witness said, she had disappeared.

When President Alfonsin was elected, promising to seek justice for the families of the disappeared ones, Coche began her own investigation. With the help of a lawyer, she discovered that two women, both matching Liliana's description, had been buried in NN graves in July 1978.

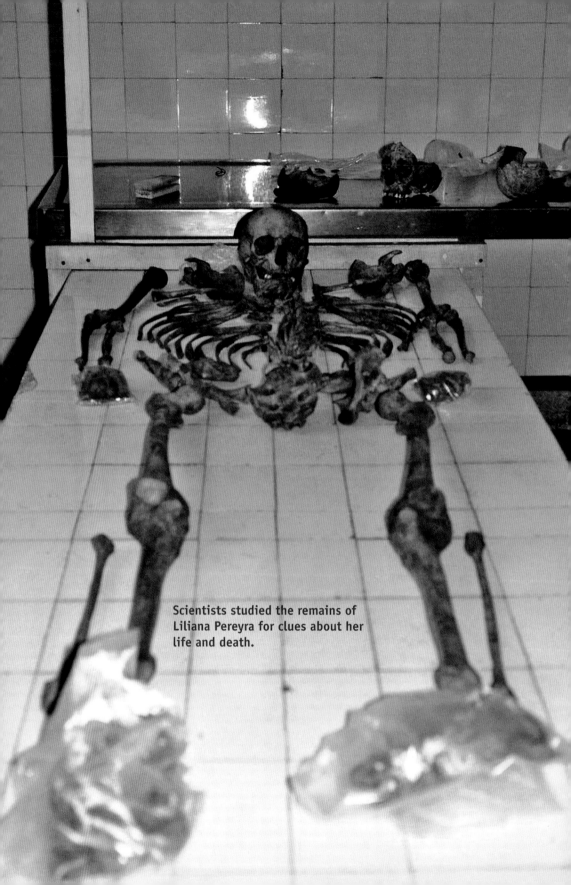

Scientists studied the remains of Liliana Pereyra for clues about her life and death.

She felt sure that one of them was her daughter. Coche had heard that there was a group of forensic scientists who could identify the disappeared ones by examining their bones. She asked if they could help.

In March 1985, Snow, the other forensic scientists, and the students unearthed a grave thought to hold Liliana's remains. For two weeks, the scientists and the students studied the bones, which told them the story of the victim's life and death. Using standard forensic anthropology measurements, they determined that the bones had belonged to a young woman of European ancestry, about Liliana's height. Levine, the dentist, found that she had had one of her canine teeth removed. They reassembled the shattered skull. Kirschner, the pathologist and an expert in gunshot wounds, could tell by the pattern of the fracture indicated that she had been shot at close range.

Although Liliana was pregnant at the time she was abducted, there were no fetal bones inside of this skeleton. A distinctive groove in the pelvis showed that the woman had most likely given birth. The clincher was in the X-rays of the skeleton. Just as no two fingerprints are alike, no two bones are exactly alike. Fitzpatrick, the radiologist, compared X-rays of the bones with those taken of Liliana before her abduction. They were a perfect match.

In May 1985, nine members of the *Junta* were brought to trial on a total of 711 charges of kidnapping, torture, and murder. This would be the first time that military leaders would be tried for past human rights abuses by a civilian government in Latin American history. The Argentine people were transfixed by the five-month trial. Clyde Snow was a witness for the prosecution. Using slides to illustrate his testimony, Snow showed how they had determined Liliana's identity and cause of death. He explained how the bones showed that she was killed at close range by a single bullet, and not in a shoot-out with the military as the defense claimed. Ending his testimony with a photograph of Liliana before her

GRANDMOTHERS OF THE PLAZA DE MAYO

Knowing that her grandson was probably still alive, Coche joined a group, *Las Abuelas de la Plaza de Mayo* (Grandmothers of the Plaza de Mayo). They took their name from the place where they gathered for years along with the mothers of the disappeared to protest and demand that their loved ones be returned. These women were determined to track down and recover the babies—more than five hundred—kidnapped from the *desaparecidos*. They combed through birth certificates and adoption papers, acted on anonymous tips, and hired investigators to find the missing children. When DNA testing became available, they compared the DNA of the grandmothers with the DNA of children suspected to have been among those kidnapped. Since 1977, the Grandmothers have found eighty-seven of the missing babies—now adults in their early thirties.

death, he said, "What I would like to point out here is that in many ways the skeleton is its own best witness."[4]

Ultimately, the court sentenced two of the defendants to life in prison. Three others received terms of 4 1/2 to 17 years. Four were found not guilty.

Justice for the Dead

Clea Koff's fascination with bones goes back to her childhood, when she would bury bodies of birds found near her home, only to dig them up later to see how long it took them to "turn into" skeletons.[5] When Koff was eighteen years old, her father, who along with her mother made documentary films about human rights issues, gave her a book that set her on the path to forensic anthropology. The book was *Witnesses From the Grave: The Stories Bones Tell*, which relates the story of Clyde Snow and the Argentine Forensic Anthropology team.

When the president of the African nation of Rwanda was killed in a plane crash in 1994, members of the ruling Hutu party launched an all-out, well-planned slaughter of the minority Tutsi people and Hutus who opposed the campaign. Although the two tribes had lived side-by-side and shared a common culture for centuries, tensions between the two populations had worsened in recent years. Goaded on by the governing party, and driven by fear, soldiers and civilians alike massacred their Tutsi neighbors. Often they were armed with little more than machetes and clubs. When it was all over, almost one million Tutsis, as well as Hutus who opposed the campaign, had been killed.

Koff was still in graduate school and studying forensic anthropology when she watched the news reports of the massacre on television. "Who's going to go over there and identify all those bodies?" she asked herself.[6] Less than two years later, she joined a United Nations team of archaeologists, anthropologists, pathologists, and others to do just that. Their

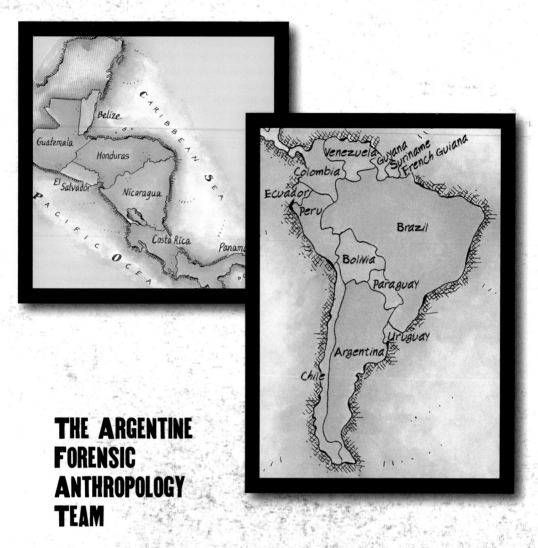

THE ARGENTINE FORENSIC ANTHROPOLOGY TEAM

After the trial of the Junta was over, the group of students who helped with the investigation became full-time researchers, forming the Argentine Forensic Anthropology Team. They continued their work of documenting human rights abuses in Argentina. Soon, the team's accomplishments began to attract the attention of human rights organizations in Guatemala, El Salvador, and other Latin American countries where similar crimes had taken place. They helped investigate massacres and trained teams of scientists how to use the forensic techniques Clyde Snow and his team had taught them. Eventually, they would be called upon to help investigate crimes against humanity all over the world.

Clea Koff uses her forensics skills to help identify victims of crimes.

goals were to identify the bodies so that they could be returned to any remaining family members, and to document that the victims had been murdered so that prosecutors could bring those responsible to trial.

Over the course of two missions to Rwanda, Koff and her colleagues excavated and analyzed the remains of hundreds of victims, many of them women and children.

Barely a week after returning home from her second mission to Rwanda, Koff left for Bosnia. A civil war in this eastern European country had left thousands of people from opposing ethnic groups dead.

She dug up bodies, many of them civilians, who had been shot, blind-folded, with their hands tied behind their backs.

Koff was able to carry out her grisly job, she said, by concentrating on the notion that she was helping provide critical evidence for the international trials where the authorities in Rwanda and Bosnia had been charged with genocide and crimes against humanity.[7]

"Part of the truth comes from the dead, whose stories are unlocked by forensic anthropologists," Koff writes. "Without forensics, mass graves of victims can easily be portrayed as mass graves of combatants."[8]

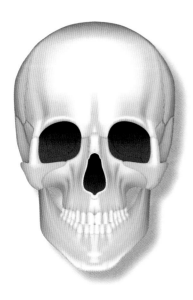

Cold Cases

Prisoners at Auschwitz-Birkenau, the World War II Nazi concentration camp, had a name for camp doctor Josef Mengele: The Angel of Death. Survivors recall a handsome man standing on a platform, whistling an opera tune as he inspected the new arrivals. With a flick of his hand, he waved the majority of them to the left—toward the gas chambers. The remainder would be put on work detail—or be forced to take part in his medical experiments.

Mengele had been trained as an anthropologist before becoming a medical doctor, and was very interested in heredity and genetic differences. Like Adolf Hitler, Mengele believed in the superiority of "Aryans," their name for "pure-blooded" Germans and northern Europeans, typically tall, blond-haired and blue-eyed. Mengele and the Nazis believed that Jews, Roma (commonly but incorrectly called Gypsies), and other ethnic groups, as well as people with mental or physical disabilities, were substandard human beings.

Mengele performed surgeries on his subjects, often without anesthesia, as well as many other grisly "experiments." Those who did not die from the procedures themselves were often killed afterward so that he could dissect and study their bodies. Not only were his experiments unspeakably cruel and evil, they weren't even scientifically sound. "He believed you could create a new super-race as though you were breeding horses," said Martina Puzyna, a prisoner at Auschwitz who also happened to be an anthropologist. "Man is so infinitely complex that the kind of strict control over such a vast population could never exist.... He was mad about genetic engineering... I believed that he would have killed his own mother if it would have helped him."[1]

By the time the Russians liberated Auschwitz on January 27, 1945, Mengele had fled—but not before collecting two boxes of papers relating to his "research." American troops captured him as a prisoner of war later that year. Not knowing that he was a notorious war criminal, they eventually freed Mengele. For several years, he laid low in the German countryside, even as some of his fellow Nazis were being tried and put to death for war crimes. Mengele became one of the most wanted men in Europe.

In 1949, after years of living under an assumed identity, Mengele managed to board a passenger ship bound for Argentina. He spent the next three decades on the run, from Argentina to Paraguay and finally Brazil. Mengele was in poor health toward the end of his life, plagued by depression and constant fear of discovery. In February of 1979, he went for a swim in the ocean, where he drowned. Mengele was buried as Wolfgang Gerhard, an Austrian friend who had given him his Brazilian identification card.

Meanwhile, the hunt for Mengele continued. People claimed to have sighted the notorious Angel of Death all over the world. The German and Israeli governments, as well as private organizations, offered large rewards to anybody who found Mengele. Finally, in 1985, the West German police uncovered evidence that Mengele was buried in a Brazilian cemetery. Many thought that it was an elaborate hoax, cooked up by his family in order to allow him to live out his last years in peace. Simon Wiesenthal, who had gained fame as a Nazi hunter, was skeptical. "This is Mengele's seventh death," he said. "Only in Paraguay has he been dead three times, always with witnesses who say it is him. On one of these occasions, we found the body of a woman."[2]

A crowd of reporters, TV cameramen, police officers, and the curious gathered to watch as gravediggers labored to unearth the body believed to be Mengele's. They smashed the lid of the coffin with a pick. In an image that would be broadcast on television sets throughout the world, a member of the Brazilian police department picked up the skull and held it high for all to see. Then, the skull and the rest of the bones were casually dumped into a white plastic tub and taken to a laboratory, where they remained under armed guard.

Clyde Snow was watching the evening news when the grisly scene appeared on his television set in Oklahoma. "They're making a carnival show out of this," he muttered to himself.[3]

Snow knew that police officers untrained in forensic techniques could easily botch such an investigation. In a television interview the next day, he said, "Having a policeman dig up a skeleton is a little bit like having a chimpanzee do a heart transplant in this case . . . small items, such as teeth, bullets, and other personal effects, which could be helpful in identification, do tend to get lost. And what you need to use is the same sort of painstaking, methodical technique that archaeologists have used for a hundred years in excavating prehistoric remains."[4]

Snow joined teams of forensic scientists from the U.S., Brazil, and West Germany to study the remains. The atmosphere was tense; Snow's comments had stung the Brazilian investigators. They knew that the eyes of the world were on this case.

The Investigation

The forensic scientists had some physical information on Mengele, based on government and military records and photographs. His records described him as a white male, 174 centimeters (5 feet 8 inches) tall. His head circumference was 57 centimeters (22.4 inches). His dental chart showed that he had twelve fillings; a photograph of the man showed that he had a gap-toothed smile. He was right-handed. While at Auschwitz, he had been involved in a motorcycle accident, although the records didn't indicate that he had broken any bones. It wasn't much to go on—but it was all they had.

The scientists gathered around the table where the bones had been laid out by the Brazilian investigators. Richard Helmer, a West German skull expert, shook his head when he saw the skull—perhaps the most critical piece of evidence. It lay in pieces, smashed by the gravedigger's shovel. Only the top part of the **cranium** was intact.

Brazilian police believed these were
the remains of Josef Mengele.

After a long silence, one of the pathologists asked, "Dr. Helmer, do you think you can reconstruct it?"

"It?" he asked.

"The skull."

"Oh . . . certainly. Yes, I can do it."[5]

Helmer, using tweezers, glue, and seemingly endless patience, worked on reconstructing the broken parts of the skull. Snow and the other forensic scientists focused on the remaining bones. Judging from the sturdy bones of the cranium and the narrow pelvis, they knew their skeleton was male. By comparing the shoulder blades and sockets, they could tell that he was right-handed. And the shape of his skull—the part that was in one piece—suggested that he was of European ancestry. So far so good. But they still had to rule out whether the bones had in fact belonged to the real Gerhard, Mengele's assumed identity.

Judging from the wear and tear on the teeth and bones, the man had been between sixty and seventy years of age when he died. Gerhard would have been in his fifties in 1979. The length of his **femur** indicated that he was 173.5 centimeters tall. Gerhard, whose nickname was the German equivalent of "Stretch," was over six feet tall. Whoever was buried in Gerhard's grave, it was definitely not Wolfgang Gerhard himself. (The scientists later found evidence that the real Gerhard died in Austria in 1978.)

A team of forensic radiologists and dentists made another important discovery. An X-ray of the skull's upper jaw revealed a curiously wide gap between the two halves of the upper palate—a sign that the man had had a gap between his two front teeth. This gap-toothed trait is an inherited condition found in just 11 percent of the world's population. The scientists glanced between the X-ray and a photograph of Mengele at the age of twenty-seven, his smile clearly revealing the gap between his two front teeth.

Helmer took just three days to assemble the pieces of the shattered skull. He glued in ten teeth and a set of dentures found in the grave and studied the skull. He studied the skull—the size of the eye sockets, the angle of the cheekbones, the width of the nasal opening. The bone structure underlying faces is what allows us to recognize individual faces, and Helmer had recently perfected a technique that would allow him to compare a skull with a photograph.

He secured pins with a dab of clay to thirty points on the skull. Each point corresponded to known places on the face where the tissues varied in thickness. He mounted it on a post next to a photograph of Mengele taken in 1938. Helmer focused one video camera on the skull, and a second one on the photograph, fiddling with both images until they were the same size. Then, he superimposed the two images.

The normally calm Helmer excitedly summoned the rest of the forensic scientists. The photograph was perfectly superimposed onto the skull, every point matching. "Now you see that this isn't fantasy," Helmer told his hushed audience. "This is Josef Mengele."[6]

The team was sure that the skull belonged to Josef Mengele, but many others remained unconvinced. Finally, investigators located a dentist in Brazil who had treated a man named Wolfgang Gerhard in 1978 who matched Mengele's description. The dental X-rays matched those of the skull perfectly.

Until They Are Home

Captain Anthony Shine, a U.S. Air Force fighter pilot, was flying his aircraft on a military patrol mission near the border of Laos and North Vietnam when he radioed his wingman, another pilot flying nearby. The year was 1972, and the United States had been at war with North Vietnam for thirteen long, difficult years. He was going to move down below the cloud cover for a closer look, he told the wingman.

DNA EVIDENCE

Although the investigators involved in the Mengele case concluded the remains in Wolfgang Gerhard's grave were indeed those of the notorious Angel of Death, some Israeli authorities remained unconvinced. In 1990, the German prosecutor in charge of the case turned to a British scientist named Alec Jeffreys, the father of what was then an amazing new technique called DNA fingerprinting. DNA is the genetic material inside every cell that determines individual characteristics like hair color, height, or the shape of your nose. Although over 99 percent of the DNA sequences are identical in all humans, a small number of them are unique to each individual. These are called DNA fingerprints. By comparing two different DNA samples, scientists could determine whether they came from the same person, related people, or unrelated people.

Jeffreys had become famous just a few years earlier when he used DNA fingerprinting to help solve a double murder case in England. Could he use DNA fingerprinting to settle the Mengele case? Although DNA can survive for a long time in bones, it tends to break down over time. With the aid of an expert in DNA extraction—"she can get DNA out of a stone, just about," Jeffreys said—he managed to get just enough DNA from the bones to study.[7] He compared the DNA samples from the bones with those of Mengele's son, who was still alive. The results were clear: The son was related to the man whose bones they'd unearthed from that Brazilian grave. At long last, the authorities closed the book on a forty-year-old war crimes investigation.

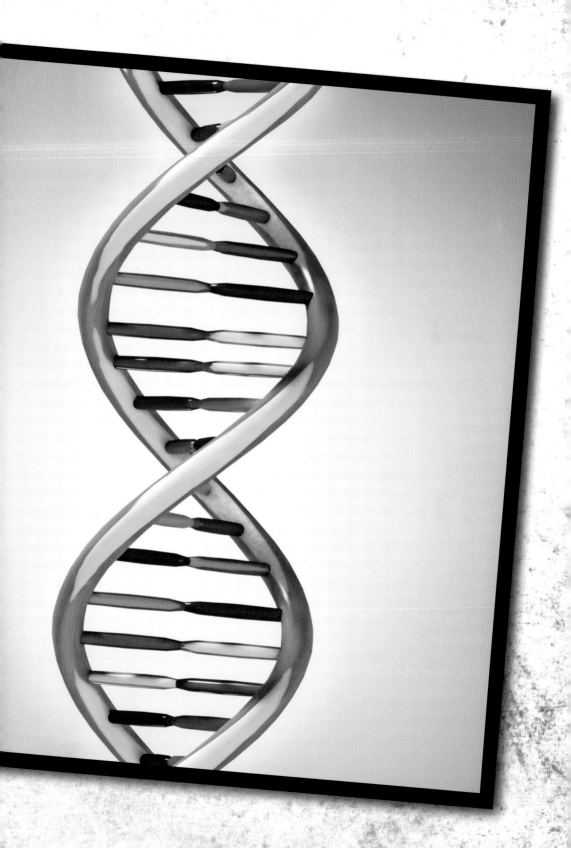

The wingman waited. After ten minutes had passed, he tried to radio Shine. There was no word. Had Shine been shot down? Ejected from his plane, possibly to be captured by the enemy? A search and rescue team carried out a two-day search, but Shine was never found. The thirty-three-year-old Shine was declared Missing in Action, leaving behind a wife and three young children in upstate New York.

The Joint POW/MIA Accounting Command (JPAC), the military unit charged with finding and identifying missing warriors, says that nearly 84,000 Americans remain unaccounted for since World War II. Over 1,700 of these were involved in the Vietnam War.[8] Based on the island of Oahu in Hawaii, JPAC scientists and investigators send out search and recovery teams all over the globe to find the remains of missing service members. JPAC's Central Identification Laboratory is the largest forensic anthropology lab in the world.[9] This is where the mystery surrounding Captain Shine would finally be solved.

Although the Vietnam War ended in 1975, it would be decades before U.S. investigators were allowed to search for the bodies of the missing service members. In 1994, a survey team from the United States and Vietnam followed a tip from Vietnamese locals who claimed they had found and buried the body of a U.S. pilot in 1972. The team found pieces of a flight suit, an oxygen hose, and a few bone fragments. Lacking the expertise of a forensic anthropologist, they closed the site, sending the bones back to Hawaii.

All the while, the family of Lieutenant Colonel Shine (he had been promoted after he was declared dead) had been monitoring the search, following any leads of their own. Not satisfied with the government's efforts, Shine's daughter, Colleen, flew to Vietnam to conduct her own investigation. She rented a jeep, hired a Vietnamese translator and guide, and headed for the crash site. With dogged determination, Colleen found a villager who had her father's helmet—complete with Captain

THAT FACE LOOKS FAMILIAR

In 2000, law enforcement officials brought the bones of a man found in the Nevada desert to the FACES laboratory at Louisiana State University. They'd had no luck in identifying the man. If they could reconstruct what he'd looked like in life, they hoped that a photo might just spark the memory of someone who once knew him.

Mary Manhein and her colleagues at FACES made some skull measurements, determining the width of the victim's nose, the shape of his mouth, his ancestry, and approximate age. Eileen Barrow, an expert at facial reconstructions, created a clay model based on the measurements. They scanned a photograph of the clay head into a computer, enhanced it to make it look more real, and posted the image throughout the area. Two women thought they recognized their brother, missing for over a decade. Scientists compared DNA recovered from the bones with DNA extracted from the sweat stains of the brother's old baseball cap. It was a match. The sisters finally laid their long-missing brother to rest.

An anthropology team sifts through ground and rock, looking for personal effects of a pilot who crashed during the Vietnam War.

Shine's name written on the inside. This evidence was enough to send another recovery team back to the crash site.

This time, they talked to the man who had found Shine's helmet. The plane, he said, had been shot down. The pilot had ejected from his seat before crashing. They found the dead pilot in a tree, and buried him in an old bomb crater nearby.

The new site was a gold mine of information: more bone fragments, the pilot's dog tag, and pieces of his flight suit. The forensic anthropologist at the site was careful to document and preserve each piece of evidence. This was important, because it was not uncommon for some Vietnamese to "plant" more recent remains in old craters, hoping to be paid for their efforts. But photos taken at the site showed live, unbroken rootlets growing into the pilot's bones—proof that the remains had been in the ground for a very long time.

But how could they be sure the bone fragments were actually the remains of Lieutenant Colonel Shine? Since the remains were so small and so few, the forensic anthropologists at the Central Identification Laboratory in Hawaii analyzed the mitochondrial **DNA** (mtDNA) in the pieces of bone (see sidebar). They compared the mtDNA from the bone fragments with the mtDNA from Lieutenant Colonel Shine's mother, brother, and sister. They found that the longest mtDNA sequence they got from the bone samples matched Lieutenant Colonel Shine's relatives. It was found to occur in less than 4 percent of samples from unrelated people—not a perfect match, but given all of the other evidence, good enough.

MITOCHONDRIAL DNA ANALYSIS

The DNA that resides inside the nucleus of every cell is what makes each person unique, and is widely used for DNA finger-printing. But DNA is easily destroyed. It breaks down over time. It is often difficult to recover DNA from old bones, or from remains that have been burned.

Not all DNA resides in the nucleus, though. Some DNA is also found in the mitochondria, those parts of the cell that serve as power generators. Mitochondrial DNA exists for one thing only: to tell mitochondria how to do their jobs. And, since it has only one job to do, it is much smaller than nuclear DNA.

But mtDNA is very useful to forensic scientists, for two reasons. First, it is very plentiful: There are thousands of copies of mtDNA for every copy of nuclear DNA. So there is often enough mtDNA left in old bones long after nuclear DNA has dropped to undetectable levels. And while nuclear DNA is a combination of genes from the individual's mother and father, mtDNA comes from the mother alone. This means that a mother and her children, the mother's sisters and her children, the mother's mother— all of the maternal relatives—will share the same mtDNA.

Today, the Central Identification Laboratory uses mitochondrial DNA analysis in more than half its cases.[10]

Lieutenant Colonel Shine was buried, with full military honors, at Arlington National Cemetery. Colleen Shine was satisfied. "The scientific evidence of these few fragmentary remains, coupled with the aircraft wreckage and circumstantial evidence, offered our family long-awaited peace of mind and heart. My mother now knew that she was no longer a wife but a widow, and my brothers and I knew that our father was not being tortured, and that he would never walk back into our lives. Dad died doing something he loved, flying, and for a cause in which he believed.[11]

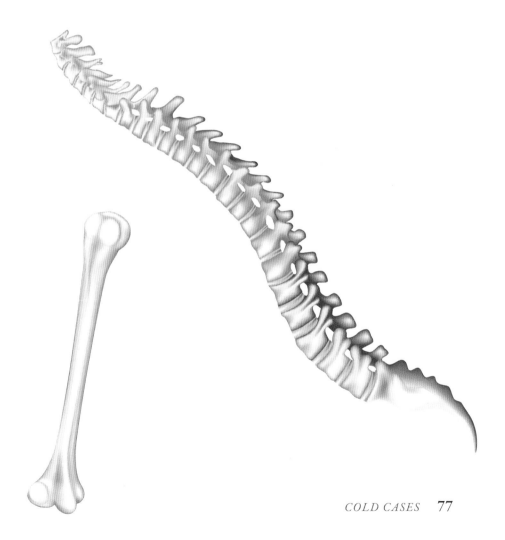

When Disaster Strikes

April 19, 1995, dawned clear and bright in Oklahoma City. By 9 A.M., the Alfred P. Murrah Federal Building was buzzing with the activity of hundreds of office workers and visitors. Children in the building's day care center were playing and eating a morning snack.

Lakesha Levy, an Airman First Class in the U.S. Air Force, was applying for a social security card at the Murrah Building. The twenty-year-old wife and mother had joined the Air Force to finance her dream of going to college and becoming a nurse. She was on duty, wearing her combat uniform. At 9:02 A.M., a van loaded with a huge bomb exploded just outside the building. Super-hot gas streaked through the building. The ground shook in a tremor that could be felt thirty miles away. The nine-story building collapsed, creating a crater thirty feet deep.

The Alfred P. Murrah Federal Building was destroyed by a bomb on April 19, 1995.

Minutes later, paramedics, firefighters, and police officers began to arrive on the scene. "In an awful way, it was breathtaking," recalled Jana Knox, an emergency medical technician. "There was glass shimmering on the streets and scrap metal everywhere."[1]

Firefighters worked feverishly to free survivors trapped in the debris. "In about fifteen minutes," Knox said, "our ambulance was almost stripped of supplies. People needing help were everywhere. I would just finish with one and turn around to find twenty more. It was like a scene out of hell, and it would be like this for hours."[2]

By the end of the day, more than eight hundred people had been treated for injuries. One hundred sixty eight people, including Lakesha Levy, lost their lives. Nineteen of the dead were children. A team of volunteer recovery specialists worked twelve-hour days over the weeks to come to find and identify all of the bodies and body parts buried in the rubble. They wanted to identify all of the victims so that their remains could be returned to their families, of course, but it was also important that they recover every scrap of evidence that might be used to solve the crime.

Agents with the Federal Bureau of Investigation who saw the crater knew almost immediately that they were dealing with a crime scene. A cash machine video camera near the building had captured an image of a yellow moving truck parked in front of the building just before the explosion. Agents found pieces of the truck, coated with tell-tale traces of the bomb-making material. Soon, agents found an axle from the truck that had held the bomb; an identification number led them to a rental agency in Junction City, Kansas.

A man who went by the name of Robert Kling had rented a van there on April 17. Several people said they had seen a second man with Kling. Using information from people who had seen them, an FBI artist quickly drew up sketches of Kling and his companions—John Doe No. 1 and

John Doe No. 2. The agents took the sketches door-to-door in Junction. City. They hit pay dirt at the Dreamland Motel, where the manager said that John Doe No. 1 had stayed there and checked out the day before the bombing. But his name wasn't Kling. It was Timothy McVeigh. And he had been driving a yellow moving truck.

Two days after the bombing, a nationwide computer search showed that a twenty-seven-year-old man named Timothy McVeigh was in jail in Oklahoma. He had been arrested ninety minutes after the bombing on a traffic violation. He had posted bond, and was scheduled for release in less than an hour. Formal charges were filed against McVeigh for murder, conspiracy, and the destruction of government property.

McVeigh hated and mistrusted the government, and had ties to anti-government groups. These groups, often heavily armed, believe the government threatens their freedom. At the time he was arrested, he was wearing his favorite t-shirt, bearing the image of a tree dripping with blood. The caption read: "THE TREE OF LIBERTY MUST BE REFRESHED FROM TIME TO TIME WITH THE BLOOD OF PATRIOTS AND TYRANTS." Police also arrested and charged McVeigh's friend Terry Nichols. They did not think he was John Doe No. 2—Nichols had been hundreds of miles away when the mystery man had been spotted with McVeigh. But they had ample reason to suspect that Nichols had helped McVeigh plan the bombing.

Rescue workers recovered the last three bodies from a massive pile of rubble on May 29. But they also found something puzzling: part of a decomposed leg. A leg that didn't seem to belong to any of the bodies they'd recovered.

Forensic experts initially thought that the leg belonged to a white male, but they weren't certain. The foot wore two dark socks and a black combat boot. The leg had been separated from the rest of the body about six inches above the knee. Pieces of plastic embedded in the bone told them that the victim had probably been very near the center of the blast. Judging by the size of the bone, the leg might have belonged to a powerful woman or an average-size man. Because the leg had been badly damaged from the blast and had lain in the rubble for several weeks, the skin had begun to decompose and discolor. The color told the investigators little about the person's ancestry.

The FBI sent hair and tissue samples to experts in Washington, D.C. There, they concluded that the individual was probably female and black, although they couldn't be certain.

Timothy McVeigh's defense lawyer found out about the mystery leg that summer. He accused the experts of lying about their findings to help win the government's case against McVeigh. The leg, he said, must have belonged to the *real* bomber—John Doe No. 2, who had been described by witnesses as a muscular white man with dark hair.

Doug Ubelaker, the FBI's top forensic anthropology consultant at the Smithsonian Institution, had an idea. He called a forensic anthropologist named Emily Craig, who had written a scientific paper showing that the structure of the knee could yield important clues about the race of an individual. Dr. Craig, who was a medical illustrator before becoming a forensic anthropologist, had long known that the knees of black people have more space at the hinge than those of white people. She had watched thousands of knee surgeries on athletes of all racial groups, and dissected hundreds of amputated legs. If anybody could determine the race of this victim, it would be Dr. Craig.

Lakesha Levy's aunt holds Levy's boot, found
in the wreckage of the Murrah Building.

"I spent a grueling but satisfying day examining every inch of the leg, analyzing tissues, measuring x-rays, and taking detailed handwritten notes," Dr. Craig wrote.[3] At the end of the day, she told the investigators that the leg had belonged to a woman of African ancestry.

The FBI soon confirmed that the leg belonged to Lakesha Levy. She had been buried with someone else's left leg—an understandable mistake given the terrible mutilation of the many body parts that had to be sorted through.

Although the identity of the leg that was mistakenly buried with Levy remains unidentified, Dr. Craig and the medical examiners on the case have confirmed that it belonged to a white female.

Whether that white female was one of the victims somehow buried without her left leg, or an unidentified 169th victim, remains unknown. What is known is that it did not belong to John Doe No. 2—if he existed.

On June 2, 1997, the jury found Timothy McVeigh guilty of the murder of 168 people. He was sentenced to die by lethal injection. His co-conspirator, Terry Nichols, was sentenced to life in prison for his part in the bombing.

DMORT

It seems that the world has suffered a rash of disasters in recent years. Some, like the bombing of the Murrah Building, are deliberate acts of terrorism. Accidents or natural disasters—airplane crashes, factory explosions, earthquakes, hurricanes, and tsunamis—can claim the lives of hundreds or even thousands in a matter of minutes.

When disaster strikes, the first priority is to save lives. But when the emergency medical teams have done all they can to help save the living, others must find and identify the dead—and that can be a staggering

job. The sheer number of fatalities and destruction can overwhelm local medical examiners or coroners.

Fortunately, there is a specially trained group of volunteers who can respond to such catastrophes: DMORT, or the Disaster Mortuary Operations Team. Forensic anthropologists join specialists in forensic dentistry and pathology; fingerprint experts, photographers, X-ray technicians, funeral directors, medical examiners, and others to identify the

DMORT teams respond to all kinds of disasters. The team seen here is removing a body from a home after Hurricane Katrina.

DISASTER ARCHAEOLOGY

Richard Gould, an anthropologist and archaeologist at Brown University in Providence, Rhode Island, visited the site of the 9/11 terrorist attack on the World Trade Center three weeks after the tragedy. Dr. Gould's trained eyes saw what the cleanup crews could not: human bone fragments among the ashy grey deposits that still covered much of Lower Manhattan. Human remains, office paper stained with blood, and other material were blown far away from Ground Zero—some as far away as Brooklyn, several miles away.

Dr. Gould knew that he could bring his skills as an archaeologist to help find the remains of people who died in the World Trade Center attack. Archaeologists study the material remains of the human past—usually the very distant past. But archaeology can be very important in recovering materials from recent disaster sites. He formed a volunteer group, the Forensic Archaeology Recovery team, to search for material related to the 9/11 attack.

"Four-and-a-half years later, they were still finding human remains in great numbers," he told a reporter. "I'm afraid they may keep finding this material for years."[5]

Disaster archaeology can be very difficult, but Gould knows that the work is invaluable. "Archaeology . . . eventually leads to what is sometimes called 'emotional closure,' when the victims' remains are returned to their families," he wrote. "Then, that terrible cloud of uncertainty is lifted, and they can begin to grieve."[6]

victims and investigate the scene. It is a critical job, both for legal reasons and to help grieving friends and families claim the bodies of loved ones.

After the September 11, 2001 attacks on the World Trade Center and the Pentagon, and the crash of United Airlines Flight 93 in Pennsylvania, the government called for DMORT teams nationwide to help local authorities locate and identify the dead. Working twelve-hour shifts, the team members sorted through the debris, searching for human remains—often very small—and other evidence that might help identify the victims. They sent the remains to laboratories, where forensic anthropologists measured and X-rayed the bones, searching for clues about the victim. Forensic dentists examined the teeth, documenting fillings or wires from braces that might be matched to dental records. They extracted DNA from the remains and compared their samples with blood samples from relatives. They compared their samples with DNA extracted from hair left in combs back home, toothbrushes—anything that might help identify the victim.

Paul Sledzik, who headed the DMORT team that worked at the crash site of United Flight 93 in Pennsylvania, summed up the feelings of his team. "It's heart-rending work, absolutely," he said. "But this [DMORT operation] has a distinct difference to it. Given what's been going on nationally, people here are extremely focused on completing the work here. They feel they can provide a service to these families and to their country and they are here to do that."[4]

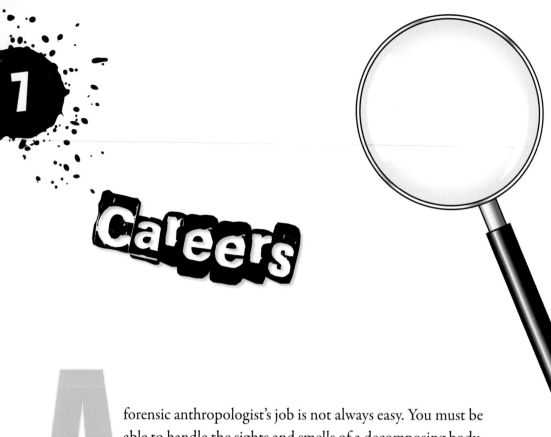

Careers

A forensic anthropologist's job is not always easy. You must be able to handle the sights and smells of a decomposing body, and be willing to get dirty while looking for clues. You may be asked to help investigate the scene of a crime on weekends or evenings. And it is often difficult to bear witness to the horrible acts that some people inflict upon others. Real forensic anthropologists are quick to point out that their jobs are not nearly as glamorous as those depicted on the popular CSI television shows.

But if you can deal with these things, a career in forensic anthropology can be deeply rewarding. You should be observant, good with details, and have a strong interest in science. You should have good speaking skills and be able to explain complex scientific ideas in simple everyday language, since forensic scientists are often called upon to testify in a court of law. Most of all, you should have a strong desire to help provide justice for those who can no longer speak for themselves.

Theresa Gotay Nugent, a graduate student in forensic anthropology at Texas State University, said that she wants to go to South America to

work on human rights cases. "Even though we're working with the dead," she explained, "we actually help the living, the families of people that are missing and feared dead. It's not all just macabre [gruesome]. You can actually make a difference doing this."[1]

You should plan on earning a bachelor's degree in anthropology or a related science, and a Master's (MS) or Doctoral (PhD) degree in physical or biological anthropology. This will take about six to ten years. During your education, you should get some practical experience working with an experienced forensic anthropologist. Physical anthropologists with a PhD and practical experience can take a series of exams to become certified as experts by the American Board of Forensic Anthropology. This is desirable but not essential.

Some colleges and universities offer a bachelor's degree with a forensic anthropology concentration, or a certificate program in forensic anthropology. This level of training would allow you to become a technician, skilled in assisting in forensic anthropology investigations.

Many forensic anthropologists are university professors. They teach courses in physical anthropology, conduct research, and consult on forensic anthropology cases when called upon do to so. The U.S. Army's Central Identification Laboratory employs forensic anthropologists to search for and recover war casualties. Other forensic anthropologists work for museums, the FBI and state bureaus of investigation, and medical examiner offices.

Forensic anthropologists with training in archaeology often help law enforcement officials recover human remains from crime scenes. They may use their knowledge of soil, plants, and insect activity to help solve the case. Some forensic anthropologists specialize in creating computer or clay models of faces based solely upon a skull.

The incomes of forensic anthropologists vary, depending on the degrees earned, the actual job, where they work, and how many hours they work. Although there are no data available for the specific area of forensic anthropology, the mean annual wage of anthropologists and archaeologists is $57,230.[2]

The following are some selected schools offering training in forensic anthropology and related fields:

Applied Forensic Sciences Department
Mercyhurst Archaeological Institute
Mercyhurst College

501 East 38th St.
Erie, PA 16546
Phone: 814-824-2000
http://mai.mercyhurst.edu/academics/applied-forensic-sciences/

Archaeology and Forensics Laboratory
University of Indianapolis

1400 E. Hanna Avenue
Indianapolis, IN 46227-3697
Phone: 317-788-3486
http://archlab.uindy.edu/

C.A. Pound Human Identification Laboratory
University of Florida, Gainesville

Turlington Hall, Room 1112
PO Box 117305 Gainesville, FL 32611
Phone: 352-392-2253
http://web.anthro.ufl.edu/capoundlab.shtml

Department of Anthropology
University of North Carolina, Wilmington

601 South College Road
Wilmington, NC 28403-5907
http://people.uncw.edu/albertm/

Department of Anthropology (Forensic Anthropology option)
California State University, Los Angeles

Los Angeles, CA 90032
Phone: (323) 343-5205
http://www.calstatela.edu/academic/anthro/forensic.htm

Department of Anthropology, Forensic Science,
& Archaeology, Baylor University

One Bear Place #97173
Waco, TX 76798-7173
http://www.baylor.edu/afsa/

Forensic Anthropology
California State University, Chico

400 W. First Street, Chico, CA 95929-0400
Phone: 530-898-6192
http://www.csuchico.edu/anth/PAHIL/

Texas State University, San Marcos
Department of Anthropology, Forensic Anthropology Center

601 University Drive
San Marcos, TX 78666
Phone: 512-245-8272
http://www.txstate.edu/anthropology/facts/

The University of Tennessee, Knoxville
Department of Anthropology, Forensic Anthropology Center

250 South Stadium Hall
Knoxville, TN 37996-0760
Phone: 865-974-4408
http://web.utk.edu/~fac/

Forensic Anthropology Program
Department of Anthropology and Sociology
Western Carolina University

101 McKee Building
Cullowhee, NC 28723
Phone: 828-227-2430
http://www.wcu.edu/3403.asp

Forensic Science Program, Sam Houston Sate University

Chemistry and Forensic Science Building
Room 221 A
Box 2525, 1003 Bowers Boulevard
Huntsville, TX 77341
Phone: 936-294-4286
http://forensics.shsu.edu/

CHAPTER NOTES

Chapter 1. An Introduction to Forensic Anthropology

1. Paul Purpura, "Detective recalls odor of death; Metairie man accused of killing his father," *The Times-Picayune* (New Orleans), September 23, 2009, METRO, p. 1.

2. Michelle Hunter, "Son tells jury that denial caused him to neglect his father's body," *The Times-Picayune* (New Orleans), September 25, 2009, <http://www.nola.com/crime/index.ssf/2009/09/son_tells_jury_that_denial_cau.html>.

3. Michelle Hunter, "Grandson testifies he thought smell in house where grandfather was decomposing was 'dead rats', " *The Times-Picayune* (New Orleans), September 24, 2009, <http://www.nola.com/crime/index.ssf/2009/09/chad_adams_whose_father_lon.html>.

4. William R. Maples, Ph.D., and Michael Browning, *Dead Men Do Tell Tales: The Strange and Fascinating Cases of a Forensic Anthropologist* (New York: Doubleday, 1994), p. 280.

5. Stanley Rhine, *Bone Voyage: A Journey in Forensic Anthropology* (Albuquerque: University of New Mexico Press, 1998), pp. 1–3.

Chapter 2. The Murderous Beginnings of Forensic Anthropology

1. Christopher Joyce and Eric Stover, *Witnesses from the Grave: The Stories Bones Tell* (Boston: Little, Brown & Co., 1991), p. 47.

2. Simon Schama, *Dead Certainties: Unwarranted Speculations* (New York: Alfred A. Knopf, 1991), p. 122.

3. Schama, p. 135.

4. T.D. Stewart, *Essentials of Forensic Anthropology* (Springfield, Ill.: Charles C. Thomas Pub., 1979), p. xii.

5. Robert Loerzel, *Alchemy of Bones: Chicago's Luetgert Murder Case of 1897* (Urbana, Ill.: University of Illinois Press, 2003), p. 24.

6. Ibid., p. 125.

7. Ibid., p. 170.

8. E. Baumann, and J. O'Brien, "The Sausage Factory Mystery," *Chicago Tribune Magazine*, 3 August 1986, pp. 16–20.

Chapter 3. The Body Farm

1. William Bass and Jon Jefferson, *Death's Acre: Inside the Legendary Forensic Lab—the Body Farm—Where the Dead Do Tell Tales* (New York: G.P. Putnam's Sons, 2003), pp. 59–71.

2. Ibid., p. 238.

3. "Forensic Anthropology Data Bank," *University of Tennessee Forensic Anthropology Center,* <http://web.utk.edu/~fac/databank.shtml> (February 21, 2010).

4. Jarrett Hallcox and Amy Welch, *Bodies We've Buried: Inside the National Forensic Academy, the World's Top CSI Training School* (New York: Berkeley Books, 2006), pp. 93–94.

5. Bass and Jefferson, p. 252.

6. Times-Picayune staff writers, "Marrero native on Mississippi death row spared lethal injection by supreme court," October 7, 2009, <http://www.nola.com/crime/index.ssf/2009/10/marrero_native_sitting_on_miss.html> (November 9, 2009).

7. Monte Basgall, "Prehistoric Cold Case Hints of Interspecies Homicide," *Duke University press release,* July 20, 2009, <http://www.dukenews.duke.edu/2009/07/neandercide.html>.

8. Steven E. Churchill et. al., "Shanidar 3 Neanderthal rib puncture wound and paleolithic weaponry," *Journal of Human Evolution*, 57 (2009), pp. 163–178.

9. Bass and Jefferson, p. 34.

Chapter 4. Human Rights

1. Gabriela Nouzeilles and Graciela Montaldo, *The Argentine Reader* (Duke University Press, 2002), p. 477.

2. Christopher Joyce and Eric Stover, *Witnesses From the Grave* (Boston: Little, Brown and Company, 1991), p. 217.

3. Jeff Guntzel, "'The Bones Don't Lie': Forensic Anthropologist Clyde Snow Travels Continents to Bring the Crimes of Mass Murderers to Light," *National Catholic Reporter*, July 30, 2004, pp. 13–16.

4. Joyce and Stover, p. 268.

5. Clea Koff, *The Bone Woman* (New York: Random House, 2004), p. 8.

6. Ibid., p. 15.

7. Perlez, Jane, "A 'Bone Woman' Chronicles the World's Massacres," *New York Times*, April 24, 2004, p. 4A.

8. Koff, p. 265.

Chapter 5. Cold Cases

1. Gerald L. Posner and John Ware, *Mengele: The Complete Story* (New York: McGraw-Hill Book Co., 1986), p. 43.

2. Ibid., p. 318.

3. Christopher Joyce and Eric Stover, *Witnesses From the Grave* (New York: Little, Brown and Co., 1991), p. 161.

4. Ibid., p. 161.

5. Ibid., p. 175.

6. Ibid., p. 196.

7. Nick Zagorski, *Proceedings of the National Academy of Sciences,* "Profile of Alec J. Jeffreys," 103(24), June 13, 2006, p. 8920.

8. Joint POW/MIA Accounting Command, *FY 2009 Annual Report*, pp. 3–5, <http://www.jpac.pacom.mil>.

9. Dawnie Wolfe Steadman, ed., *Hard Evidence: Case Studies in Forensic Anthropology* (Princeton, N.J.: Prentice Hall, 2003), p. 109.

10. Central Identification Laboratory, < http://www.jpac.pacom.mil/>. (February 26, 2010).

11. Steadman, p. 288.

Chapter 6. When Disaster Strikes

1. "The Story of the Oklahoma City Bombing," p. 14, April 19, 1995: 9:02 A.M. *The Official Record of the Oklahoma City Bombing.* (Oklahoma Today Magazine: 2000 Revised edition).

2. Ibid., p. 21.

3. Emily Craig, *Teasing Secrets From the Dead* (New York: Crown Publishers, 2004), p. 236.

4. Cindi Lash, "Flight 93 victim identification long, arduous," *Pittsburgh Post-Gazette*, September 25, 2001, <http://www.post-gazette.com/headlines/20010925sledzik0925p3.asp> (February 26, 2010).

5. Lucy Middleton, "Laid to rest at last," *New Scientist*, March 22, 2008, p. 42.

6. Richard Gould, "9/11: A Disaster Redefines the Meaning of Archaeology," *Dig*, February 2007, p. 9.

Chapter 7. Careers

1. John Burnett, "In Texas, a Living Lab for Studying the Dead," *All Things Considered news story*, National Public Radio, aired June 30, 2009, <http://www.npr.org/templates/story/story.php?storyId=105479033>.

2. Bureau of Labor Statistics, U.S. Department of Labor. Occupational Employment Statistics, *Occupational Employment and Wages*, May 2009, 19-3091 Anthropologists and Archeologists, <http://www.bls.gov/oes/current/oes193091.htm> (October 26, 2009).

GLOSSARY

anthropology—The science of the origin, development, and culture of humans.

archaeology—The study of past human life through the excavation of sites and the artifacts and other physical remains left behind.

autopsy—The examination of a body to find out the cause of death.

cadaver—A dead body; usually of a person. Term usually refers to a body used in dissection.

coroner—A public official whose chief duty is to discover the cause of death, especially one that might not be due to natural causes.

cranium—All of the skull except for the mandible, or jawbone.

DNA—Deoxyribonucleic acid. The molecule, usually located in the nucleus of the cell, that carries genetic information.

decomposition—The decay of plant or animal matter.

enzyme—A protein made by living cells that can bring about or speed up chemical reactions.

femur—The thighbone.

fingerprint—The pattern created by the ridges on the skin of fingers or thumbs when pressed onto a surface.

forensic—From the Latin *forensis*, "of a forum, public." Of or relating to the application of scientific methods and techniques to investigate a crime.

hyoid—A tiny, horseshoe-shaped bone in the neck.

maggot—The wormlike larva of a fly, commonly found in decaying matter.

pathologist—A medical doctor who specializes in the causes and effects of diseases or of injuries to the body.

pupa—The third stage of the life of an insect, between the larva and adult stages.

taphonomy—The study of what happens to organisms after they die.

vertebra—One of the sections of bone that make up the spinal column.

FURTHER READING

BOOKS

Bass, Bill, and Jon Jefferson. *Death's Acre: Inside the Legendary Forensic Lab—The Body Farm—Where the Dead Do Tell Tales*. New York: G.P. Putnam's Sons, 2003.

Craig, Emily. *Teasing Secrets From the Dead*. New York: Crown Publishers, 2004.

Ferllini, Roxana. *Silent Witness: How Forensic Anthropology Is Used to Solve the World's Toughest Crimes*. Buffalo, N.Y.: Firefly Books, 2002.

Hallcox, Jarrett, and Amy Welch. *Bodies We've Buried: Inside the National Forensic Academy, the World's Top CSI Training School*. New York: Berkley Books, 2007.

Joyce, Christopher, and Eric Stover. *Witnesses From the Grave: The Stories Bones Tell*. New York: Little, Brown and Company, 1991.

Koff, Clea. *The Bone Woman: A Forensic Anthropologist's Search for Truth in the Mass Graves of Rwanda, Bosnia, Croatia, and Kosovo*. New York: Random House, 2004.

Manhein, Mary H. *The Bone Lady: Life as a Forensic Anthropologist*. Baton Rouge: Louisiana State University Press, 1999.

Mann, Robert, and Miryam Ehrlich Williamson. *Forensic Detective: How I Cracked the World's Toughest Cases*. New York: Ballantine Books, 2006.

Ubelaker, Douglas, and Henry Scammell. *Bones: A Forensic Detective's Casebook*. New York: Edward Burlingame Books, 1992.

INTERNET ADDRESSES

History Detectives: Forensic Anthropology
    http://www.pbs.org/opb/historydetectives/techniques/forensic.html

University of Tennessee Forensic Anthropology Center
    http://web.utk.edu/~anthrop/index.htm

Visible Proofs: Forensic Views of the Body
    http://www.nlm.nih.gov/exhibition/visibleproofs/index.html

Written in Bone: Forensic Anthropology at the Smithsonian
    http://anthropology.si.edu/writteninbone/forensic_anthro_
    smithsonian.html

Lafourche Parish Public Library
Thibodaux, LA

INDEX